Plants & T

A plant is a young tree.

A plant starts its life as a seed and grows into a tree.

Quick Fact

Trees grow from the top, not from the bottom as is commonly believed.

A plant has many parts like the stem, roots, flowers, fruits and leaves.

Quick Fact
Trees lower air temperature by evaporating water from their leaves.

Leaves

Each leaf is like a kitchen of a plant where it makes food for the whole plant.

Flowers, vegetables and fruits

Flowers help in giving birth to new plants. Fruits and vegetables form food for many birds, animals and also human beings.

Quick Fact
The world's largest flower is Rafflesia. It grows in south-east Asia and weights up to 1 kg! It has a horrible smell.

Roots help a plant in absorbing food and water from the soil.

The stem carries water and food up from the roots and distributes it to all the parts through branches.

There are many types of trees. Some are tall and some are short.

Trees that live for just one season are called annual trees.

Quick Fact

A White Cedar in Canada is thought to be the slowest growing tree as it has grown less than 4 inches in 155 years!

Trees that live for two seasons are called biennial trees.

Trees that live for many seasons are called perennial trees.

Trees give us oxygen to breathe.

Quick Fact

Trees cut down noise pollution by acting as sound barriers.

They help to form clouds which give us rain!

Quick Fact

Trees and plants make their food through a process called photosynthesis.

They give us fruits and vegetables.

Quick Fact
The world's tallest tree is a Coast Redwood Tree in California.

Birds, squirrels and some snakes make their home on trees.

Quick Fact
There are about 20,000 types of trees in the world.